Second Edition

The Seer's Journey

The Path to Enlightenment

Almine

Published by Spiritual Journeys LLC

Second Edition – November 2013

Copyright 2009

MAB 998 Megatrust
By Almine
Spiritual Journeys LLC
P.O. Box 300
Newport, Oregon 97365

US toll-free phone: 1-877-552-5646

www.spiritualjourneys.com

Manufactured in the United States of America

ISBN 978-1-936926-74-9 Softcover

ISBN 978-1-936926-75-6 Adobe Reader

Table of Contents

Endorsement

"What a priceless experience to be able to catch a glimpse into one of the most remarkable lives of our time. This book is bound to have an indelible impression."

Ambassador Armen Sarkissian,
Former Prime Minister of Armenia,
Astrophysicist, Cambridge University,
United Kingdom

About the Author

Almine is a mystic, healer and teacher who for years traveled through many countries, empowering thousands of individuals drawn to her comprehensible delivery of advanced metaphysical concepts. In the wake of her humility and selfless service, unspeakable miracles have followed.

In her life, made rich by the mystical and the holy, she has stood face-to-face with many of the ancient Masters of light, with full memory of the ancient languages of the gods, in written and spoken form.

Her teachings are centered on the idea that it is not only possible to live a life of mastery and love, but that it is the birthright of every human to attain such levels of perfection. Her journey has become one of learning to live in the physical, maintaining the delicate balance of remaining self-aware while being fully expanded.

*When we live in the moment we live in
the place of power, aligned with eternal
time and the intent of the Infinite.
Our will becomes blended with that
of the Divine.*

Almine

The Seer's Journey

Long and passionate has been my journey to understand the meaning of life. I sought it in communion with nature, fasting in the deserts and in the high mountains. I looked for it in the eyes of the sage and the fool, but found in them only the images of myself.

My search brought many answers but the questions never ceased. All roads led around and around but always back to myself. As I lay in my blankets in the mountains of Montana, I saw that all stars turn through the wheel of the night except for the North Star — immovable and serene upon its heavenly throne.

Thus, like many before me, I entered the stillness within where the voice of my questioning mind was silenced. The rivers flowed within me. I was the wind and the wild horses that raced across the prairies. The bliss was deep, swallowing all desires. No boundaries did I know. Laughter rippled through my cells. I tasted divine ecstasy like honey in my palate.

But deep in the languor of my expansion, a question echoed through my soul. The dream had left the mind of the dreamer, but had the dreamer not now entered the dream? I had become still, like the North Star, but had expanded to include the movement within.

Yet again as I lay upon my bed, watching all life move within, I heard the faintest whispering: life is a journey, not a camp. As addicted as the masses are to their contracted point of view, so too is the sage who in his bliss becomes all things.

The seer in his searching through perception grows in power, ever climbing higher. To the master in enlightenment who seeks no more to understand, personal power sifts through his fingers like a fistful of sand.

The spiraling journey of the seer, the flat expansiveness of the sage — to live where these combine was for me the next stage. Memories of childhood and laughter once more returned. The adventure of the unknown, of distant horizons that beckon, was renewed.

Yet the child cannot return to the womb nor can the river return to its source. Through re-entering the drama of the human condition and again enacting my part, I knew that though the play had value, I was not the actor in the role.

From an eagle's perspective, I could view life and simultaneously see like the snail. I lived in the eye of the storm, in rest within activity. Divine discontent led me onward. I knew there must be more questions yet unanswered, something yet unseen.

All that lived in cosmic life dwelled within my being. All answers within the realms of form had already been seen. Like the winding trails I'd traveled on Earth, I now mastered time and space. Journeying into hidden realms where few seers dare to go, among demons and angels, dragons and gods, wanting to learn what they know.

Each had a page in the Book of Life, yet a great discovery did I make: within the heart of humankind, the whole Book was hidden away.

By self-centeredness obscured, all cosmic knowledge lies within humankind. The densest of all beings, man is the microcosm of macrocosmic life.

Enticing it is to discover and play amidst the wondrous realms of light. But around and around, like a fish in a bowl, is life within that which is known.

Wheel of Perpetual Regeneration

Time is a tool rather than a reality. It helps sustain the illusion of form. In timelessness, the tyranny of the appearance that form is solid releases its grip.

I chronicled my journey, not considering whether some would believe or others would scoff at my words. Like an explorer adrift on an endless sea, I charted the realms beyond mind, hoping to leave the keys to the gates that imprison mankind.

The glory of life, revealed in its parts, nevertheless seemed unreal. In a world of mirrors we live and a growing discontent did I feel. Through freedom from mind we escape our confines and can more clearly see. But behind space and time and the illusion of form lies more that is unreal.

Beyond all previous boundaries into realms of timelessness where even the illusion of the moment falls away, I searched for infinity's end. The fields of my body cracked from the strain when I saw the mirrors endlessly repeat.

The cracks caused by pain and anguish of heart a great blessing did bring. More light could I hold, more clarity gain as I transfigured into immortality.

Totally silent became the mind, like a lake lying undisturbed in the moonlight. Writing and speaking automatically occurred, unmarred by a single thought.

The languages of the kingdoms, the secrets of subatomic building blocks of life — all that I needed to know appeared. The searching through the cosmos no longer served a need.

As I sat before my fire or walked a busy street, the heavens would open. Great wonders would I see. The multiple layers of mirrors that surround our cosmos were no more than layers of a membrane, like those that in skin are found.

Clusters of cosmoses as vast as ours along a spiraled path did lie. Twelve more spiraled pathways of cosmoses I did find. A cluster they make, one of many that into eternity lie.

No need to travel through realms of mystery. Nothing seemed closed to me. My body transfigured into immortal mastery.

Wheel of Atlantean Angels

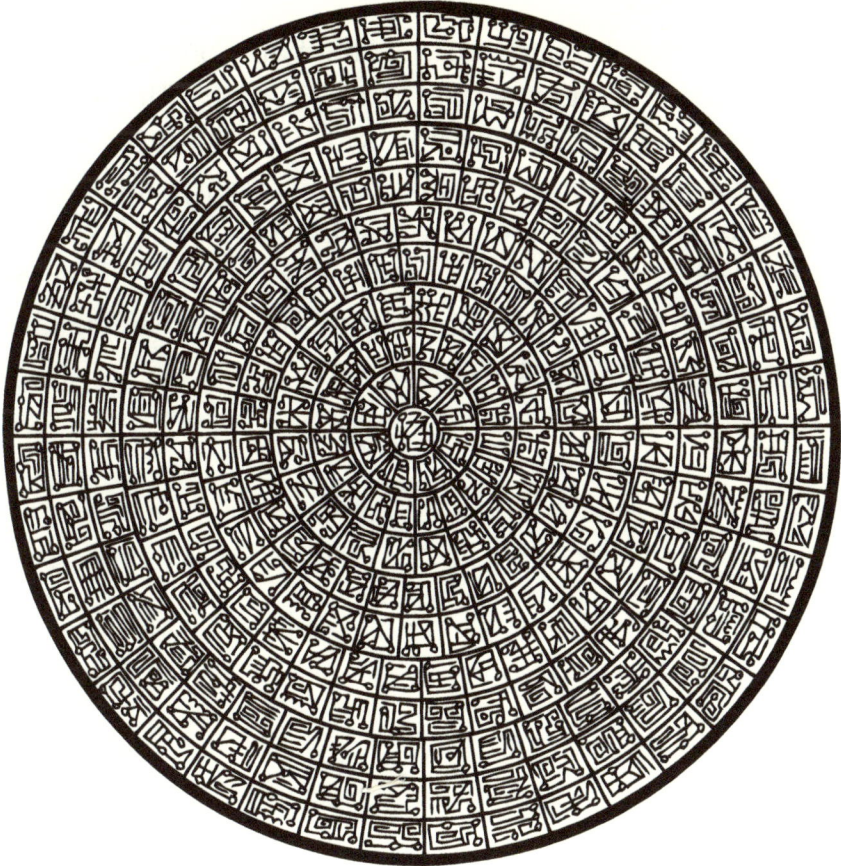

*The moment is defined by what it is not. All that is
definable is unreal.*

As I learnt and observed from what I could see, profound were the answers that presented themselves to me. Vast as the spirals that into eternity expand, they were but reflections of a DNA strand.

If one were to stand in a hall of mirrors, an infinite progression of images recedes in all directions. The slightest movement affects all. Thus it is with life. All of the grand, sweeping changes of ever-unfolding reality are but a projection through the smallest building blocks of life.

Through the heart of the subatomic particles of life shine the images of the unfolding changelessness of the One Life. This was the nature of the Dream.

Wheel of Lemurian Angels

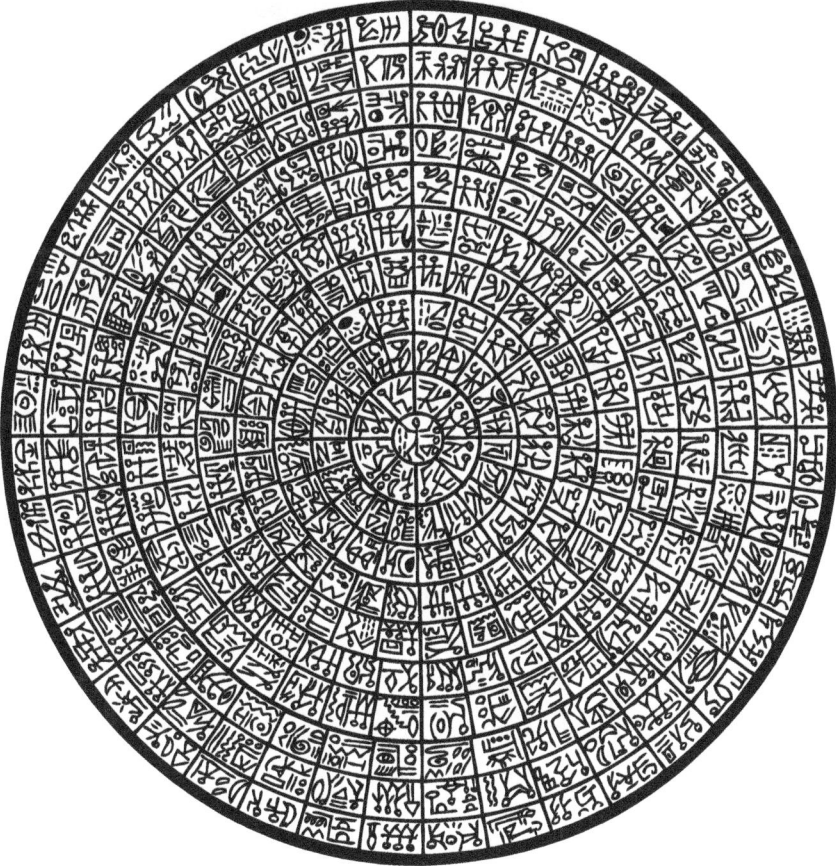

*Through the building blocks of life, the Infinite illuminates
the cosmic unfolding on an endless stage.*

Through the vastness have I peered, but mirror images were they. Like all mirrored images, the opposite of what is, did the never-ending reflections convey.

Now through the hearts of the subatomic particles, the smallest windows into Eternity, did I look. My folly was there revealed. There is no vastness or smallness; no inner or outer, for opposites cannot exist separately from each other.

Within the outer the inner resides. Within the awakening the dream abides. Within cosmic unfolding, eternal changelessness lies. I searched for the many within the One, but all I could find was me.

But in the mirror I clearly saw that diverse life forms danced upon the stage of life. How could there not be another? Where did their beauty go?

Deep in my heart these words were whispered: "The beauty you saw was yours. Never can the ocean's vastness be divided or defined. There is only One Being in existence that in formless forming expresses. The mirror you imagined, like a finger pointed at the self, showed you that which you are not, that you yourself may know."

Then unreal too my form must be, defined by what is not. The stage upon which I dance my life, by the tiny building blocks formed, likewise an illusion is. Am I then a hollow bone that never really was?

"Without the hollow bone, you never can create the flute. The breath of Infinite life through the flute, exquisite music makes."

Unencumbered then shall I dance. No self-reflection shall I seek. For mirrors could never show the One Life that spontaneously moves through me. Within the confines of illusional form, gratitude will I feel, knowing it serves the One Life's purpose of spontaneous creativity.

All life is the unknowable. There is nothing to understand, nothing to strive to become when we are an expression of the One. Yet the creation is the Creator. In the One Life no relationship can there be. Embracing the contradiction is living a life of peace.

Wheel of Merging Realities

The Scrolls of Infinity

How far have I searched, how high have I flown, finally the peace of surrender to know? Through the One Life created – this cosmic home where I am all things, yet ever alone.

But with our wings we must also have roots with which to enjoy the things of Earth. The sacred libraries with gifts most profound can, by those who can see, in many lands be found.

Hear now their wisdom, long preserved. Buried are they beneath the sands of the Earth.

Scroll of Infinity 1

The Scroll of Infinity 1

What is immortality but the prolonging of a long-forgotten dream? The search for permanence is the folly of mind, clinging to structure, refusing to leave the past behind.

When silence and movement become one within, immortality can be sustained indefinitely. But to stay the same without fluidity is, within the One Life, an impossibility.

Yield not to death but master life and change then your form like the clouds in the sky. In the dance of the rain or the river's flow, let the dance of life through you unfold.

Scroll of Infinity 2

The Scroll of Infinity 2

Let the body not rule, but master its needs. The body is a tool, a transient field floating in the spaceless space of Infinity. All that around us we see, until we affirm its existence, is only a possibility.

The body lures us into thinking we know. It gives the illusion of a reference point within eternal flow. Like the feet of a dancer, it must obey. In ecstatic union with the Infinite, the dancer's dance is not his own. No success or failure can he claim, but only the at-oneness with the One Life.

Scroll of Infinity 3

The Scroll of Infinity 3

The one who thinks he knows is captured within the chrysalis of the known. The one who lives within the unknowable flies free like the butterfly.

The illusion of the known keeps us in an earthbound perspective, like the caterpillar crawling upon the leaf, unaware that above him the butterfly dances on the wind. To such a one, life's possibilities pass by unseen.

No matrix or program or structured outcome can exist. Those are the illusional offspring of the Great Trickster — rational mind. Tricked by the senses and beguiled into thinking life is predictable, life may appear definable. Instead it is newly unfolding in its expression.

Scroll of Infinity 4

The Scroll of Infinity 4

Through the weaving of belief systems we have created a web of sub-creations. The threads of our beliefs stem from our attempts to control life by creating and defining reality.

Creation is an illusion — a mere imagining. It is when we believe it to be real that the play forms an illusory reality. Nothing new upon the stage of life can be created for the changeless and the changing dwell as one within Infinite Life.

The illusions, like shadows on the wall, are conjured by our not seeing that we need not create life, but participate in its endless suprises.

Scroll of Infinity 5

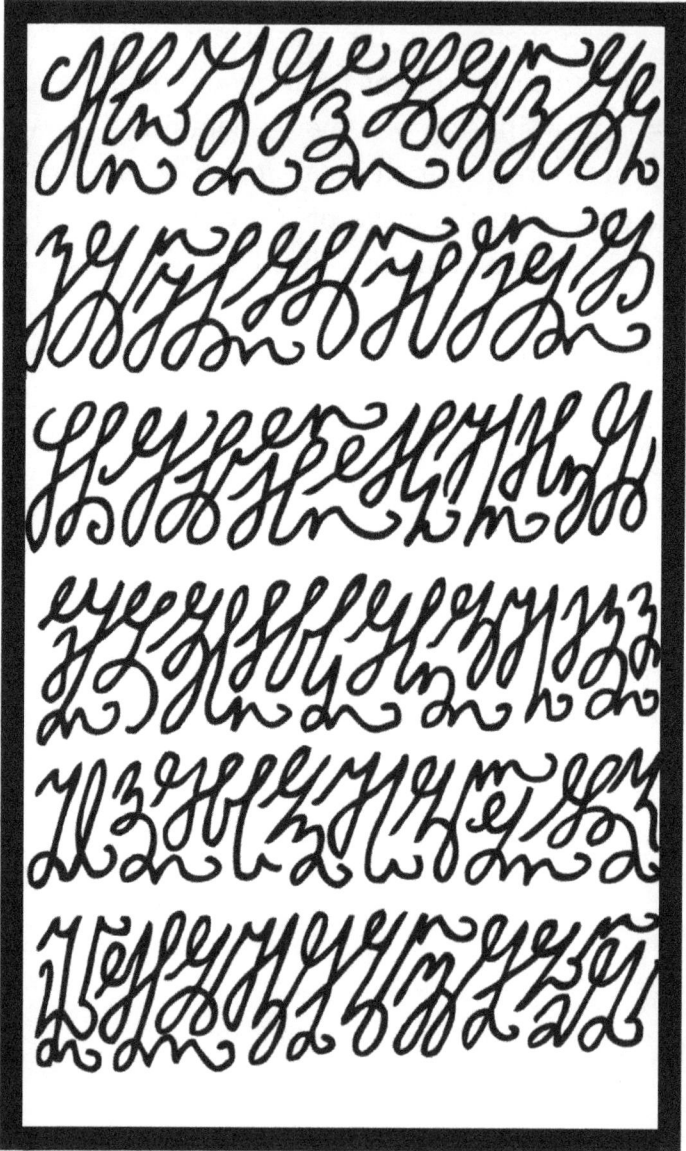

The Scroll of Infinity 5

That all things have a beginning, it has been assumed. That a point of origin precedes creation holds dual illusions: for naught has been created and nothing has been begun. Eternally we have resided, expressing as the One.

Seek not the origin of life. Succumb not to the addiction to know. For mind fixates upon certainty and resists the motionless, unknowable flow.

There is no linearity, no cause and effect, when we dwell in timelessness as the One Eternal Being.

Embracing Formlessness

And many, newly awakening in the dawn, who wished from the dream to be free, gathered to ask what their hearts would know — how life was more than it seemed ...

Almine

Why is it so, when there is more than one seen, that all must exist as only One Being?

As you awaken from life's dream, a formless form in life's endless sea, new tools are needed for spaceless space; to dance with the One Life in a paradoxical embrace. Let multi-sensory perception the five senses replace. When the need to know dissolves, effortless knowing takes place.

Then shall you taste the breath of the wind. The sound of the music you shall see. You shall hear the feelings of another's heart like music on the breeze.

But why do our eyes see spatially and our vision divide and deceive?

The deception in the vision is because of deception that is believed. We think that form is static, that it is reality that we see.

How from such deception can we ever then be free?

By throwing off the shackles of thinking that we know; by living like a child, exploring the unknown.

And tell us now of speech ... for that which is affirmed is that which comes to be.

When receiving communication, do not listen with your ears. Let all senses and the heart behind the communication hear. Assimilation cannot happen when thoughts are in the mind. When thoughts are stilled, the true intent behind language you will find.

Is language an obsolete tool for capturing reality?

You may as well catch a falling star — or reach for eternity.

Then why do we not from speaking refrain if there is nothing to be gained?

The only language anyone hears is the One Life's eternal song. Where only One Being in reality exists, communication does not belong. Communication is part of life's great conspiracy. In order to dance, it pretends duality.

But is language then a friend or foe when it filters others' words?

Play the game that life designs, but remember nothing can be heard …

What is the point of playing the game when it is only truth I seek?

Seek not that in which you dwell. Truth is the Infinite's Being. The game you play is for your sake, from appearances to set you free. Without pretense there is no dance of individuated forms. From pretending there is relationship, diverse expression is born.

Tell us of the cycles of life, of that which went before.

Imagined stages of a Dream, nothing more.

But are we yet in cycles that endlessly repeat? Perhaps just larger than those we previously had seen?

Cycles come from linear time that spirals round and round. Wherever that is encountered, cyclical change is found.

Then is there naught to change when in changeless change we dwell? What is our responsibility? Please, these answers tell.

There's no responsibility needed on your part when the Infinite unfolding flowers through your heart.

But surely when in Oneness I reside and in still surrender I remain, it assists in dissolving for all illusion's domain?

There is only perfection; even illusion plays its part. There is nothing to improve. Just live authentically through the heart.

Why is perfection not apparent and chaos seems to reign? Why is there seeming lack and many still in pain?

From a smaller vantage point a higher order cannot be seen. It appears as chaos created haphazardly. Pain comes from the impossible we attempt to do; to oppose the dance of the One Life. Through our resistance, pain ensues.

What message would you give us as you part from us this day?

You cannot leave that which you are. We are One and the same ...

The Seer's Wisdom

When the directions come home to the heart and
linearity is no more, we become the door of everything.

Courage is only needed to override the objections of the
mind. When the mind is still, right action is automatic.

The Earth is my cradle and the sky is my blanket.
Wherever I go, I am home.

The mind creates mirrors, then fights against them.
When I wait in stillness, all life reveals itself to me.

Life changes, yet does not change. In its unfolding, one form yields to another. Though it may seem destructive, there is only spontaneous perfection.

What we look at we solidify. What we experience unfolds into endless possibilities.

What is real is incorruptible and changeless. Through
the falseness of form, the real shines through and the
One Life glows.

When action has no agenda, doingness and beingness
become one. Restful repose slumbers in my work. Work
becomes work no more.

Beauty can only be seen when the mind is still and the
heart is open. What is beauty but the momentary
glimpse of Eternity?

Wherever there is division, there is illusion. Whenever
something can be defined, it is unreal.

Knowing life to be a dream, we can become lucid dreamers, masters of the dream environment. Reality becomes fluid rather than static and a life of miracles ensues.

Living in no-time does not mean that you do not pay attention to what is before you, but that what is before you is all that is.

The initiate knows he can change his environment by
changing himself. The master knows no difference, but
enjoys his environment as himself.

The need for external laws to govern inner man implies
that he is an effect of circumstances rather than the
expression of the One Life.

Community can be a blessing or a chain that binds. It is only a tool meant to serve the individuals within it, not a tyrant demanding they wear the mask of conformity.

The body is a dispensable field that can be replaced by another. It is but a servant. The real part of us is the master.

Environment can serve as a reflection of what we are
because it is us. It is just a peculiarity of our vision that
we see it as separate.

Self-confidence comes from the ego-identification of the
smaller self. Self-trust comes from knowing our
infallibility as the One Life.

Mercy comes from guilt. Guilt comes from judgement,
and judgment comes from an inability to see that
anything that exists serves a purpose or it would not
be there.

When we look back, the past comes alive in the present.
When we look forward, we create a future with only the
possibilities of the moment and without the contribution
of moments yet to come.

To live beyond the boundaries of mortality, we must live
from the core of our being and as a presence as vast as
the cosmos having a human experience.

For total Oneness to exist, all beings must be
androgynous, their masculinity and femininity blended
into one in a perfect harmonious union.

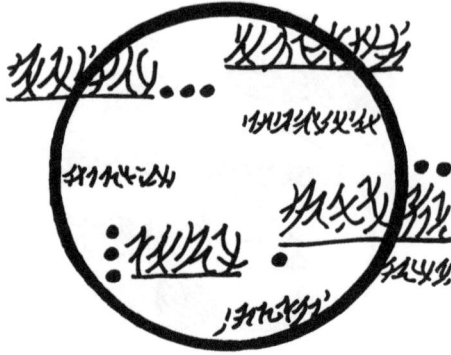

All programmed behavior must dissolve in the fluid
expression of the Infinite through us. This includes
the conditioned expectations of how to express
maleness or femaleness.

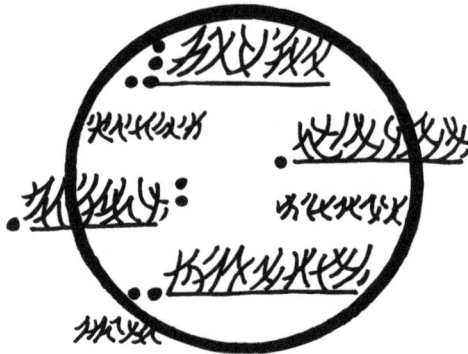

Embracing all as possible occurs when all definitions
and expectations dissolve.

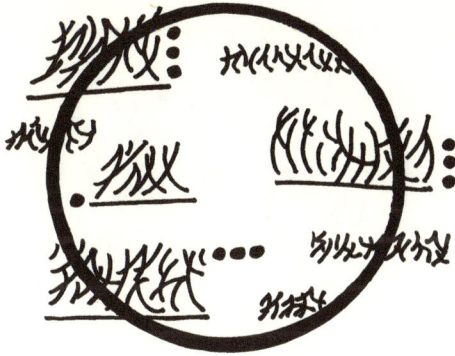

As conduits for the flow of Infinite resources, we should view ourselves as custodians rather than owners.

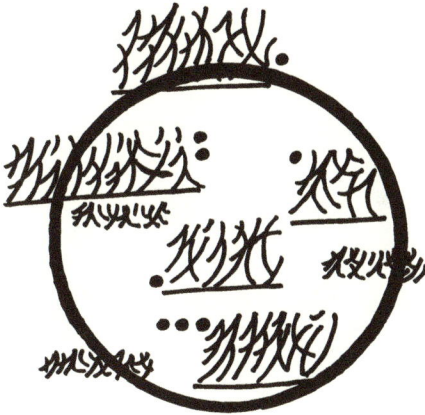

In at-oneness with the One Life, we cancel out illusion in our environment, always dwelling in sacred space.

What is the Dream of life but the unsung notes that
slumber as potential in the music?

Value illusion's role for that which is not seen, for the
gifts it brings becomes distorted in its expression.

Individuation comes from the shadows that surround
that which is illuminated by the One Life.

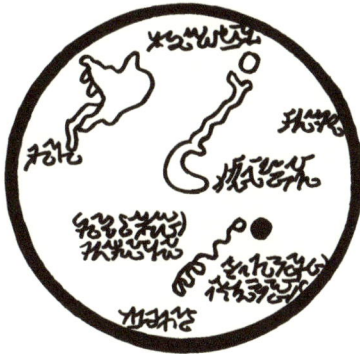

Healing duality does not mean ending the song by
playing all the notes at once, but by having each note
that is played reflect the whole within it.

Even if the illusory form should die, as long as we
know without a doubt that we are not that which is
corruptible, another shall immediately form in its place.

No one is truly free who wears the mask of identity. He
becomes a puppet in the hands of others.

As spider webs catch a moth, so do programs catch the
human soul. Free yourself from them with vigor.

Life's song becomes discordant when we focus on
illusion, the unsung notes of life. Our focus makes
them change from potential sound to actual
inharmonious tones.

When we live from the fullness of Infinite Presence,
only the illusion that supports the dance remains. That
which trips the grace of the dancer dissolves.

Beauty seen with the eyes is the illusory beauty of
form that, like the clay pot, delights today and
fragments tomorrow.

When change is linear, we are moved out of the
innocent purity of timelessness by reaching for future
potential. When change is exponential, future potential
comes now.

When beauty is seen with the heart, we connect the real
part of ourselves to the real part of life. We enter into
the One Life.

Thought keeps the past in place, like calcifications that
constrict the present. Only by replacing thought with
effortless knowing do they dissolve.

Form and time are connected like two wings of the
imaginary bird of linear progression. When we live
in no-time, we become unattached to form.

Abundant resources become ours when we leave the
movement of life, which is time. When we become the
still point, all comes to us.

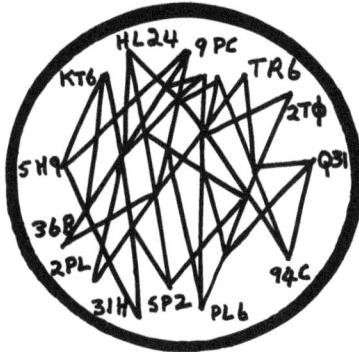

Regrets come when we believe we have had success and
failures. As a part of the One Life's Dream, life simply
flowed through us.

Our little selves have no freedom of choice. All of life is
directed by the One Life. The only way to be free is to
become the One Life.

Causes within the Dream do not create an effect. The
One Life does. When we cease trying to affect life,
miracles flow through us.

We believe we can change independently from our
environment. But we are all things. When we change,
all changes.

Density does not exist. One area of the ocean cannot be
more dense than another within the indivisibility of life.

Peace in the world comes from peace within. Peace
within comes from the inner marriage of our masculine
and feminine into perfect oneness.

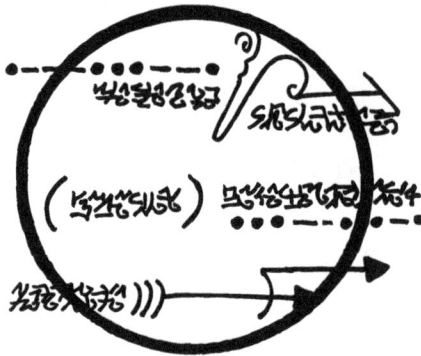

When we try and fix life we are resisting life, which
judges and divides. Acknowledging wholeness uplifts.

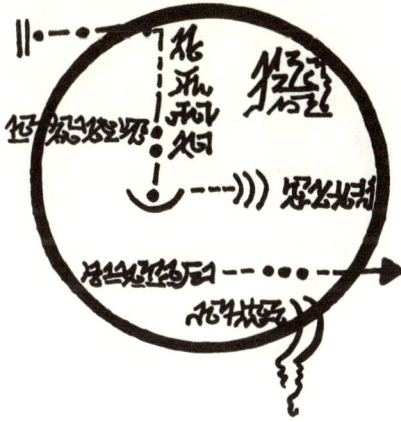

Deterioration is only present when there is opposition to life. The true nature of life is incorruptible.

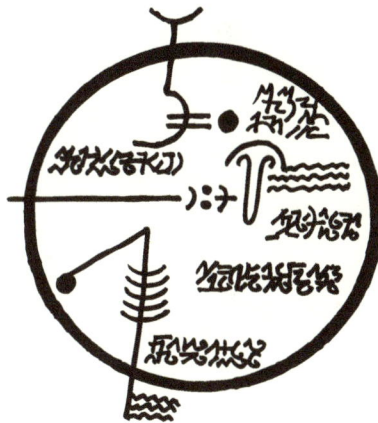

There can be no such thing as order when it is defined as structure. It is only a tool of control created by the mind.

There can be no such thing as chaos. No flaws in the
One Being exist. Chaos is but the way we describe that
which defies our understanding.

All-knowingness is not available through mind but
comes as the effortless and spontaneous expression
of the heart.

At no time does life require that we understand it. The
One Life knows all, and from our small perspective,
it is incomprehensible.

Any relationship is an illusion within the One Life, even
the inner relationship of the observer and the observed.

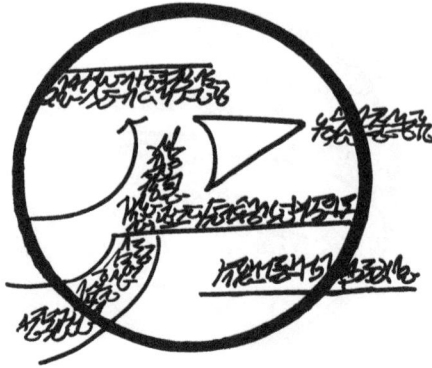

Self-reflection obstructs the purity of spontaneous living
by creating self-relationship.

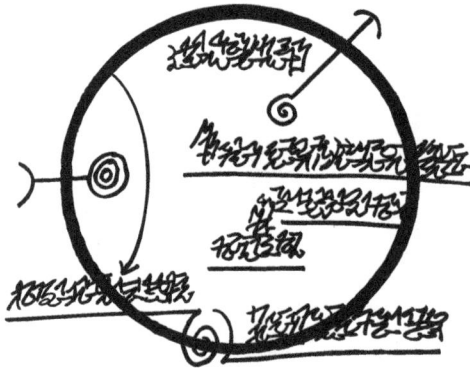

The all-knowledge and skill of the One Life is ours
to draw upon. That learning is needed to accomplish
excellence is an illusion.

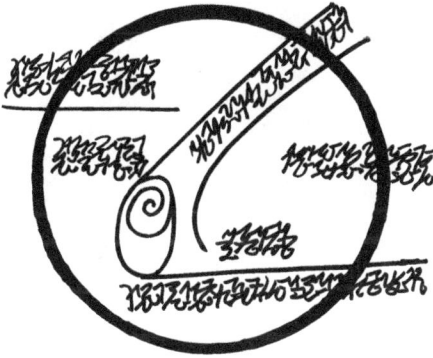

Life around us lies in intermingled fields of possibilities
that come alive only when the song of our lives
stimulates them into existence.

Unfoldment seems as movement, but that is just an
illusory trick of the senses. There is no movement
because there is no space or direction in the Being
of the One.

All levels of consciousness are equal in their
contribution to the One. The same perfection flows
through the sage and the fool.

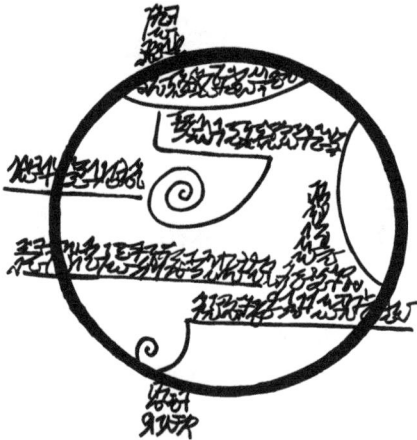

The flow of life is not movement. That is an illusion due
to successively accentuating ever-existing fields like the
notes played on a piano.

Many value knowledge and seek it above all else.
But what is knowledge but the static perception of
yesterday's unfolding life?

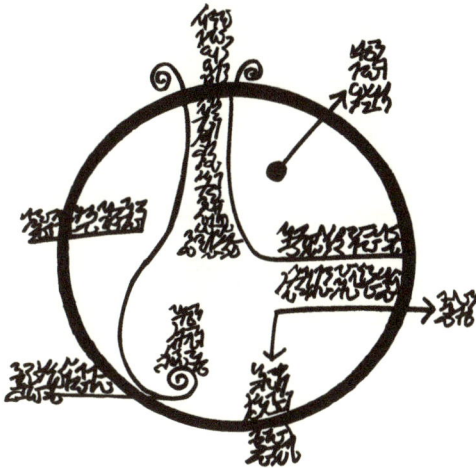

There can be no hierarchy of knowledge when it is
defined as the effortless knowing of the moment — a
gift available to all.

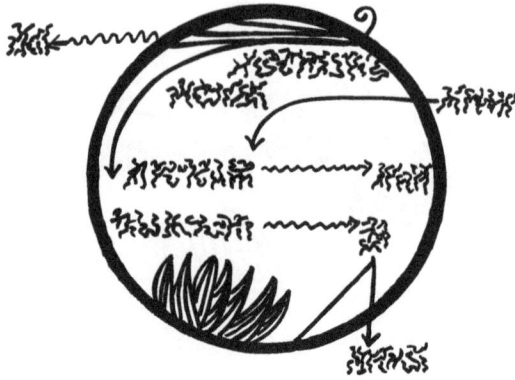

Beauty that reflects the unobstructed expression of the
One Life cannot change or fade.

There cannot be a hierarchy of beauty when each
individuated life form expresses a unique facet of
unfolding life. The lily can be no more beautiful
than the rose.

Beauty, as the true expression of Infinite Life, must
renew itself in timelessness. The cosmos does not
support the static.

When loved ones succumb to death, we may not be able
to communicate between realms, but we can within the
Oneness of our Being. Death cannot separate that.

In acknowledging the oneness of man, all diverse
perspectives of the tribes of humanity become ours
and we become wealthy within.

We think we carry the weight of the ages, but to the
One Life, only a moment has passed.

The key to stepping off the moving wheel of linear time
into the stillness of the One Life is to release the concept
of relationship through the understanding that there is
only One Being.

Layers of illusion will not release until their value is
seen. Acceptance is the beginning of change.

Separation has brought comfort to the parts of Creation developing at different speeds. Recognize this, for separation to yield to Oneness.

The changing of the cosmos from a caterpillar into a butterfly may seem catastrophic, but only from Infinite vision can the perfection of the changes be seen.

The Dream has refined the cosmos in its incubation
stages. The tools of the Dream were space and time.
These can now be released with gratitude.

There is no point of origin or arrival. There is no need
for haste or striving when life is seen from this eternal
perspective.

No approval from others can ever be valid, for they
cannot understand the unique perspectives and
contributions of our lives.

No self-approval is needed for we have been created
for the sake of joy. There is nothing to accomplish other
than deep enjoyment of life.

Opposition must be gratefully acknowledged as the tool
of Individuation. It is that which has enabled the joyful
dance of relationship.

Nothing has ever been out of control in life. It just seems
so from our small vantage point.

Truth is all that exists and it is the foundation of life.
Illusion is the temporary tool of truth.

Hierarchies divide unless we realize that we are both
the high and the low points of life; the high notes and
low notes of the symphony.

We often feel responsible for maintaining harmony in our environment. From the large picture there is only harmony, thus nothing to maintain.

Contemplate the flawlessness of life and it will reveal itself to you in endless synchronicities.

The shadows in our lives are nothing more than the
tricks we play on ourselves to express previously
unyielded potential.

Whether we struggle toward awakening or permit it
to come effortlessly, every understanding comes at the
exact moment intended by the One Life.

Through us, the One Life expresses flawlessly and
in spite of ourselves. The gentlest violin and the
thunderous drums have equally important parts
in the symphony.

Life is a perfectly directed play and every being plays
his part. Even if there is seeming apathy on the part of a
character, it is written into the script.

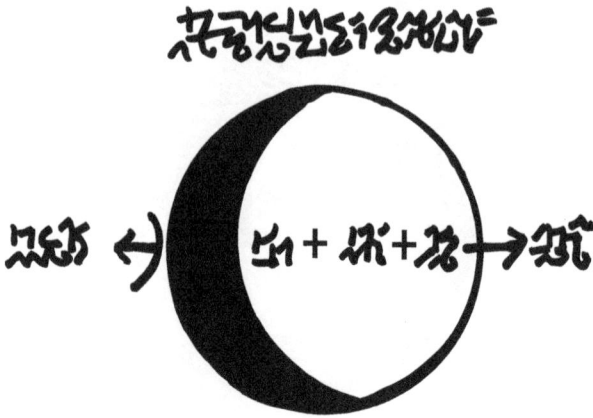

Life spins on a single point. Each of us is such a pivot point, impacting the whole with every action in every moment.

Size means nothing to the Infinite who dwells in spaceless space. Because we see the world as large and ourselves as small, we think the world can impact us. In our reality, as a gateway for the One Life, we are the cause, not the effect.

The seeming happiness of some living on the treadmill of life is an illusion. Happiness is not fulfillment of our desires, but fulfillment without having desires.

We hesitate to act before we can ensure a beneficial outcome. All outcomes are beneficial in the benevolence of the Infinite.

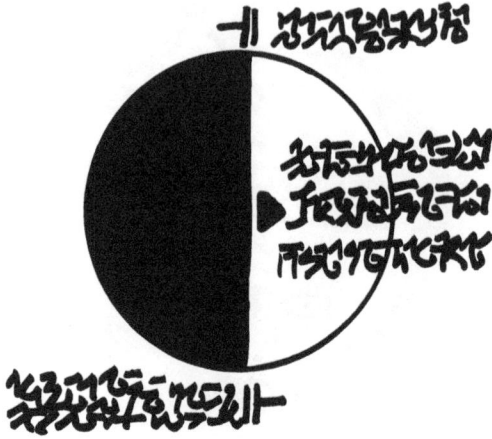

Let life unfold through us spontaneously and guilelessly, cradled in the knowledge that life is benevolent to all individuations.

Surrendering to the solitariness of finding there is no being other than Ourselves, transitions us to the eventual fullness of knowing Ourselves to be all things.

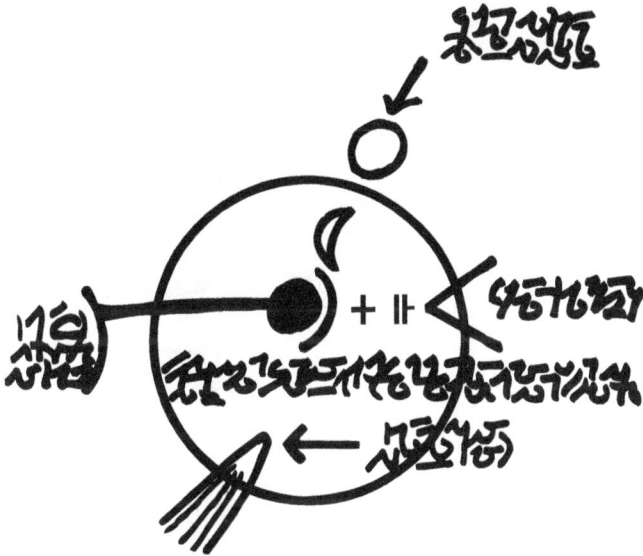

All comfort zones consist of the familiar and the known, whether one is in ego-identification or the mastery of expansion. Life must become the unknowable to become one with the Infinite.

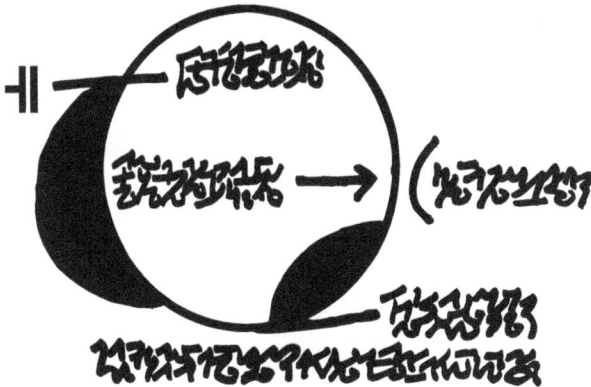

There is no growth needed, but neither can there be stagnation. Stagnation must yield to the exuberant gushing forth of the One Life.

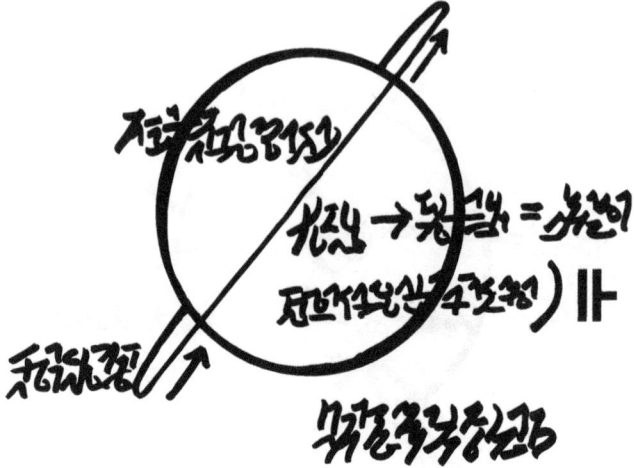

It is within the innocent discovery of life that the master is born. Let our mantra be: *I know nothing. I experience all things in the timelessness of my being.*

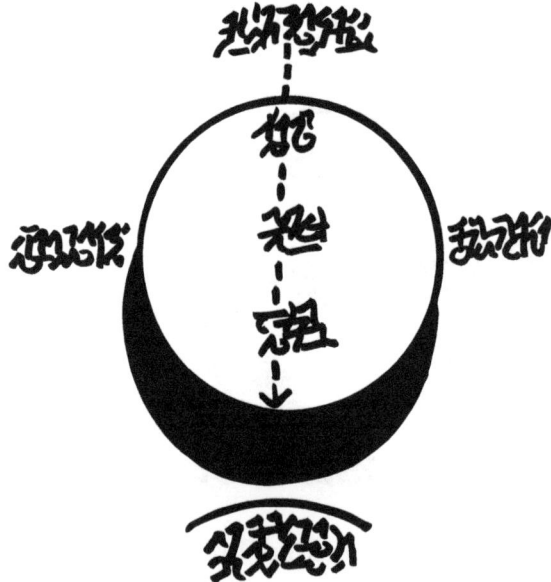

The tendency to label parts of life in order to pacify reason and provide the illusion of predictability, enslaves us to form. To circumvent this, we experience life with complete attention to the now.

The more we focus on one thing to the exclusion of others, the more limited life becomes. To focus on any part of life is to attempt to hold a gushing fountain in a bucket.

We are like doorways for Infinite compassion. To love others before self-love is not possible because it is self-love that opens the door of the heart.

Other than Divine Compassion, all types of love are but the sub-creations of man. Human love binds, Divine Compassion sets all potential free.

When we do not live with acknowledgement of the interconnectedness of life, the fragmentation of the self causes the madness of egocentricity.

Conviction does not equate with accuracy. Yet many follow blindly because they are deluded into thinking they can know when life is essentially unknowable.

Genius has no intellect. It is present in the master with emptiness of mind as effortless knowing.

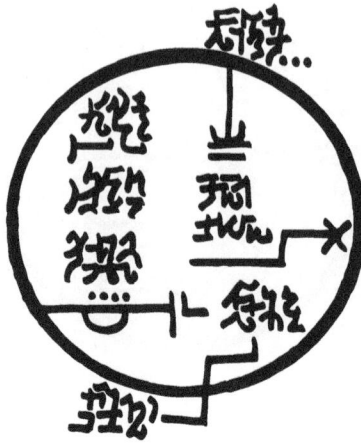

The fear of making mistakes, coupled with the
realization that life is unknowable, causes man to cling
to fragments of yesterday's truth. It is in self-trust as the
One Being that we release the obsolete.

We think we procrastinate but the cosmos   unfolds
with immaculate timing. We are always exactly on time.

The timing of the dance of life is orchestrated by what
seems like delays. But flawless is the timing of the steps
of the dance.

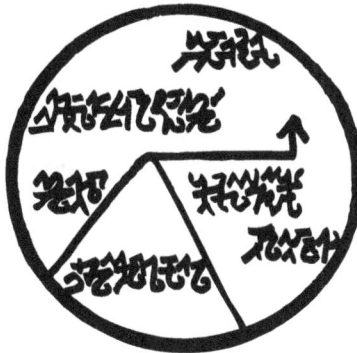

The deep seated fear that the One Life may behave
destructively comes from seeing the destruction of the
old as cataclysmic. From the large, eternal perspective,
life yields gracefully to unfolding.

The ocean of consciousness that each one is, does not
bemoan its losses or rejoice in its gains. The ocean
in its fullness, ebbs and flows in an endless expression
of itself.

Like a wayward child that challenges the authority of
the One Life's guidance, watch with benign humor
the antics of mind; but, like a wise parent, do not
indulge them.

In the play of life, those who are the planetary light
bearers also play the role of life's archetypal pivot
points. This subliminal knowledge can urge them to
save the world, but life effortlessly pivots through them.

Because life moves through us, we have no freedom
of choice and hence no responsibility. The concept of
freedom is like the hand saying to the body, "I want to
be free".

The tribe is one of the timing mechanisms of life. It tries to bind with conformity, keeping individuals in mediocrity. Those who wish to live in excellence must break free from the tribe.

Yesterday's wisdom ended yesterday's dream. It has very little application to ending the dream of today.

If you feed the tiger, it will take your hand instead. It is
not moral to pacify and indulge the unreal.
It is dysfunctional.

The existing unfoldment of life is not noticeable because
all life moves and changes at once. This creates no
reference point by which to measure change. Life is
completely new each moment.

In the quest for the discovery of the self, some seek it in others. The sage seeks it in the metaphysics of the cosmos. Both are equally valid in revealing the never-ending mystery.

Self-knowledge precedes self-love. But the only self-knowledge we can ever have is that we are an infallible and pure instrument of the One Life.

Karasu hura
tranit blivesh-
pi' urananat krava

Erchba mivet hersene?
usetvi blahes esenech-
vi' aranat truhesvabi'

Kiranat pliset bla-
vi minech haras
esevetvi'

The more we strive for enlightenment, the stronger the
pull to keep us down. Levitation must be balanced by
gravitation. Only in changeless change is there
no polarity.

Kaabavach
nenes heret usa-
klet vivavesbi'saru

Kasava nechsavi' barut
mishavach serut uraspi
belevich hirasut mirach

Kespahur setnahut
brishpa hechvi'

To maintain the unfoldment of the One Life, our efforts
to bring illumination to life increase the illusion of
beings of shadow. In this way, the cosmic symphony
is always in harmony.

"There are no beings of shadow", says the teacher of the known as he swims around his unreal fishbowl of light. "There are unreal beings of shadow", says the teacher of the unknown as he creates them by accessing the unyielded potential they represent.

Creation is a dream, for in the One Life individuation can never be. In full cooperation with the Infinite, it becomes a pleasant dream.

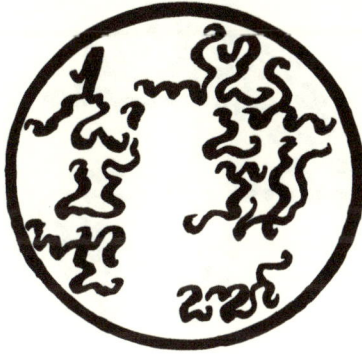

Structured programs of living, such as social conditioning, act like a virus to life, causing a dissonant reality. Observe the origins of your actions that they are not from programming.

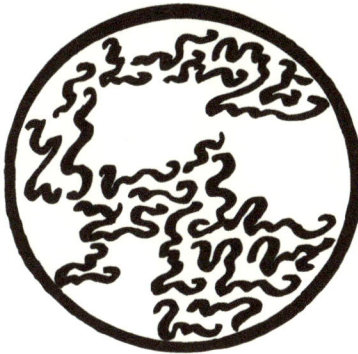

As long as any programming exists in our lives, our feelings are unreliable sources for conveying the One Life's unfoldment through us.

There is no destiny or fate. No divine mission we need
to fulfill awaits us. It is the tyranny of reason that
demands we justify our existence beyond the joy
of living.

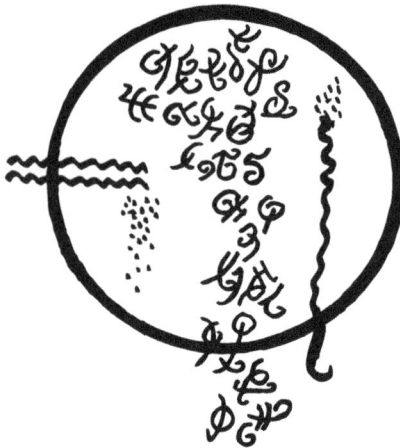

Many believe there are key moments we must seize in
order to maximize the opportunities of life. Because life is
unpredictable, they can only be seen retrospectively and are
the unstoppable changes in pace of the One Life.

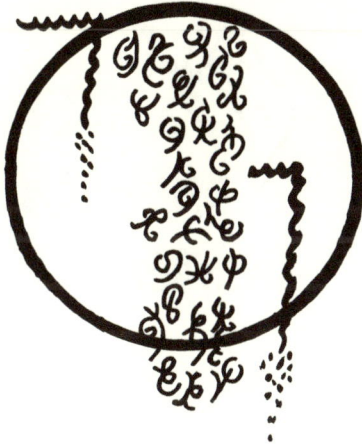

Propriety is nothing more than another's values
censoring our actions. Let freedom from concern over
others' judgments and opinions be a conscious decision.

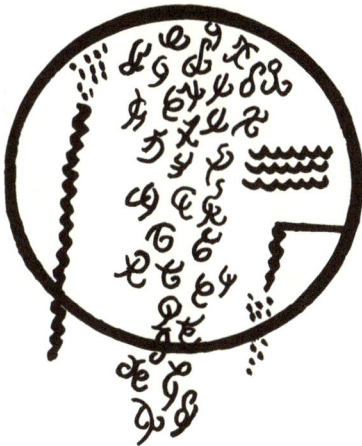

Speech without authenticity empowers the masculine,
separative qualities of life. Speaking from the heart
promotes inclusivity.

Many persuade by activating the subliminal tones of
the voice through conviction. To prevent yourself from
falling prey to this, listen with detachment.

The language of one who conveys facts is dead. The
words of one who speaks from the heart are alive. This
is because they contain the full spectrum of tones.

KLUHA – SEREBA
ANUNAT

Speak only when your heart prompts you to do so. Only
then will your words be androgynous in nature. In this
way, you speak the language of Infinite Life.

Let your speech be a cause rather than the effect of
another's speech. It is masterful to respond and
foolish to react.

Do not defend yourself. What need is there for one who dwells in the innocence of the One Life to prove that it is so? Nothing but innocence exists.

The one who speaks cannot listen. Life whispers its mysteries into the ear of one who listens in silence.

There are those who speak in circles and those who speak in a straight line. Listen to the meaning behind the circle and feel the meaning behind the obvious of the straight line.

Many programs designed by mind, such as religion, have reduced the value of the body. These are tools to control the indescribable wonder of the body.

The body in its true state is not subject to death. Only when its light is not coupled with luminosity can it die. Luminosity expresses through authentic living.

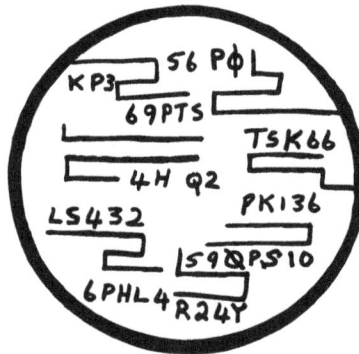

Reincarnation occurs because we shun parts of life. We then vacillate throughout lifetimes between that which we shun and that which we embrace.

When we live a programmed life, like a moth in a spider web, we cannot tell when another strand of subliminal programming captures us. Freedom from conditioning will reveal the intrusion of another's thoughts.

Let there be no regrets over right actions. Any action taken from authentic living benefits all involved, whether that is clear or not.

The more we see the divinity within others and the
more we acknowledge oneness, the more their unique
gifts become ours.

As life moves through us, its dance can be performed
with enjoyment or resistance. Enjoyment comes from
a sense of adventure and the contentment that results
from surrender.

No history exists. No future awaits. Just the moment
that stretches into eternity.

Solitude is the beginning of greatness. It is the place
where we meet the Infinite One.

From loyalty, blindness is born. See others in your
environment anew each day, that you not keep them
captive by indulging their folly.

All that has gone before has brought you to the
perfection of the moment, the beginning of timelessness
and the birthplace of Eternal Life.

Closing

Bless the chains that have bound you the way the caterpillar in gratitude receives the shelter of his chrysalis. In incubation have we lain, awaiting our entry into the majestic presence of the One Life.

Like the butterfly that takes flight upon the wind and spreads its wings in the rays of the sun, remember not your confinement with regret. It has been the womb of your birth into incorruptibility.

No more shall you see your reflection upon the walls of your confinement, nor gaze upon the distorted image of your old identity. For that which you have become cannot be defined by the limited reference point of your old, Earth-bound existence. No more do you slumber within the cocoon of half-forgotten dreams. You have merged with the grass dancing with abandon in the wind. The child and the parent of the One Life are you.

Other Books by Almine

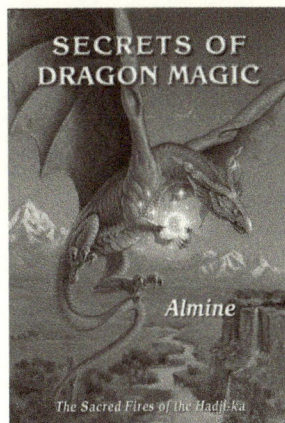

Secrets of Dragon Magic
The Sacred Fires of the Hadji-ka

This extraordinary record of the philosophy and practices of dragon magic is unmatched in its depth of knowledge and powerful delivery. From the *Sacred Records of the Hadji-ka*, kept by the dragons of Avondar, the secrets of Kundalini are revealed, designed to restore the innate, natural magical abilities of man lost by the separation of the spinal column and the pranic tube. The reader is swept along on a profound and mystical journey that pushes perception beyond mortal boundaries. Almine's infallible ability to empower her reading audience is clearly felt throughout the pages of this book.

Published: 2013, 418 pages, soft cover, 6 x 9, ISBN: 978-1-936926-56-5

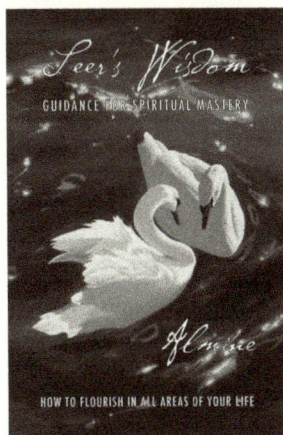

Seer's Wisdom
Guidance for Spiritual Mastery

Immerse yourself in the true nature of your being: Abundant living. This book shows you how to access your natural abundance and remove all blockages of flow. It is packed with over 400 pages of classic Almine aphorisms. Seer's Wisdom reminds you of the benign source of your own being and focuses your attention on attaining abundance: Abundance in yourself, abundance in your environment, abundance in your relationships and much more.

"To live within the Infinite's Being is to live in the fullness of an inexhaustible supply. Acknowledging the never-ending Source of abundance increases its accessibility."

Published: 2013, 430 pages, soft cover, 6 x 9, ISBN: 978-1-936926-52-7

Irash Satva Yoga

Yoga, as a spiritual and physical discipline has been practiced in many variations by masters and novices for countless years and is universally accepted as one of the most effective development tools ever created.

Man's physical form in its original state was meant to be self-purifying, self-regenerating and self-transfiguring. Through pristine living and total surrender, it was possible to open gates in the body that would allow life to permeate and flow through it; indefinitely sustaining it.

In Irash Satva Yoga, received by Almine from the Angelic Kingdom, this ancient methodology is exponentially expanded and enhanced by incorporating the alchemies of sound and frequency.

Using easily mastered postures paired with music from Cosmic Sources created specifically for each, the 144 cardinal gates in the mind and body are opened and cleansed of their dross and debris, allowing the practitioner to tap into the abundance of the One Life.

Published: 2010, 94 pages, soft cover, 6 x 9, ISBN: 978-1-934070-95-6

Other Books by Almine

Shrihat Satva Yoga

The human body is unique in that it is an exact microcosm of the macrocosm of created life. There are 12 points along the right, masculine side of the body and the same number on the left side. These are microcosmic replicas of the macrocosmic cycles of life.

The yoga postures are designed to open and remove the debris from these points – the gates of dreaming. This will occur physically through the postures and the music. Dissolving debris also occurs by way of dreaming (triggered by the breathing and eye movements), releasing past issues that caused the blockages in the points

Published 2010, 108 pages, soft cover, 6 x 9, ISBN: 978-1-934070-15-4

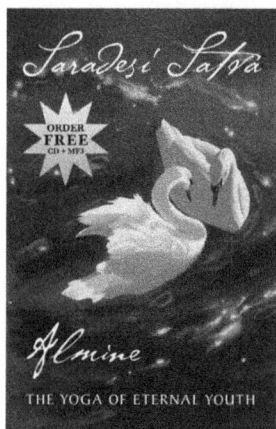

Saradesi Satva Yoga

The Yoga of Eternal Youth

As translated from the ancient texts of Saradesi – The Fountain of Youth. The ancient texts speak of time as movement. They affirm that time and space, movement and stillness, are illusions. To sustain any illusion requires an enormous amount of resources. This depletion of resources causes aging and decay. The illusion of polarity, the impossibility that the One Life can be divided and split is brought to resolution by balancing the opposite poles exactly. Only then can they cancel one another out, revealing an incorruptible reality that lies beyond – the reality of Eternal Youth.

Published 2011, 115 pages, soft cover, 6 x 9, ISBN: 978-1-936926-05-3

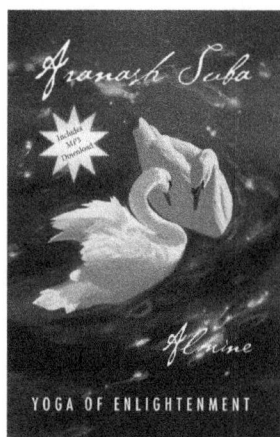

Aranash Suba Yoga - The Yoga of Enlightenment

Almine's yoga for releasing trauma and strengthening the Eternal Song of the Infinite within.

Aranash Suba Yoga works at a deep core level to assist with releasing trauma, specifically through the effects that the postures, meditations and stretches have on the psoas muscle. This yoga turns its back on the illusions of the matrices and embraces the contradiction of an existence of no opposites. The overall benefit of *Aranash Suba Yoga* is to release the hold of illusion and strengthen the Eternal Song of the Infinite within.

Published: 2012, 116 pages, soft cover, 6 x 9, ISBN: 978-1-936926-50-3

Other Books by Almine

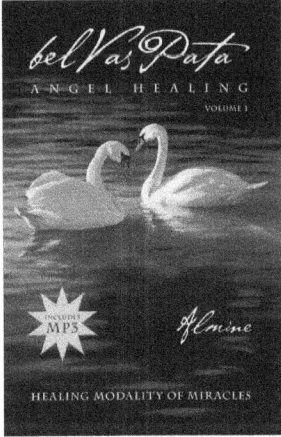

Belvaspata, Angel Healing, Volume I
The Healing Modality of Miracles

Whether you are a beginner or an experienced master of the miraculous healing modality of Belvaspata, this comprehensive guide is an information rich handbook that will serve as your most valuable tool – a compendium of information for everything you need to know to establish yourself as a practitioner of this miraculous healing modality of the angels. Also included are Kaanish, Braamish Ananu and Song of the Self Belvaspata.

Published: 2011, 394 pages, soft cover, 6 x 9, ISBN: 978-1-936926-34-3

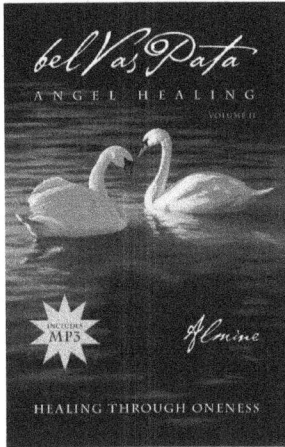

Belvaspata, Angel Healing, Volume 2
Healing through Oneness

Fairy Sound Elixir MP3 included

Whether you are a beginner or an experienced master of the miraculous healing modality of Belvaspata, this comprehensive guide is an information rich handbook that will serve as your most valuable tool – a compendium of information for everything you need to know to establish yourself as a practitioner of this miraculous healing modality of the angels. Belvaspata Volume II includes "The Integrated Use of Fragrance Alchemy," which delivers the method to obtain wellness of the emotional, mental and physical bodies through the combined use of Belvaspata, the alchemy of fragrance and the Atlantean Healing Sigils.

Published: 2012, 467 pages, soft cover, 6 x 9, ISBN: 978-1-936926-40-4

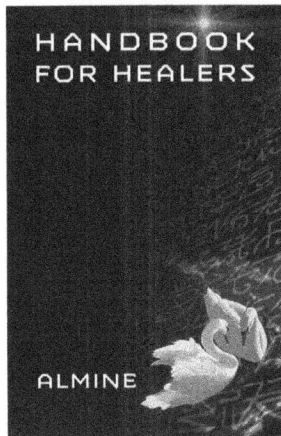

Handbook for Healers

The Healing Wisdom of the Seer Almine

Handbook for Healers is an invaluable tool for anyone interested in self-healing or the healing of others. It offers both practical and spiritual guidance gleaned from the globally acclaimed Seer Almine's advice to her students during the past decade. It reveals vital information on rejuvenating the body and understanding its communication through the language of pain, and many more empowering insights.

Published: 2013, 648 pages, soft cover, 6 x 9, ISBN: 978-1-936926-44-2

Other Books by Almine

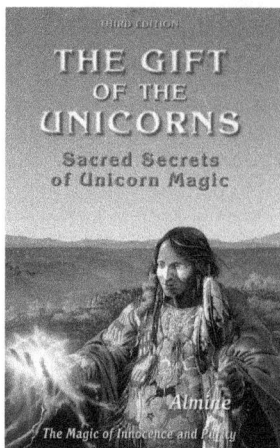

Gift of the Unicorns

Sacred Secrets of Unicorn Magic, 3rd Edition NEW

Where have the Unicorns gone? And, what about mystical winged horses, mermaids, and giants – do they exist? The answers to all of our questions about these fabled creatures can be found in The Gift of the Unicorns.

This magical book tells the story of the Unicorns and Pegasus, and their heroism in preserving purity and innocence during the ages of darkness on Earth. In their own words, these beings reveal where they went, the purpose of their golden shoes and the sacred mission they undertook for the Mother of All Creation. What's more, they share long-held secrets about the Earth.

Published: 2012, 188 pages, soft cover, 6 x 9, ISBN: 978-1-936926-48-0

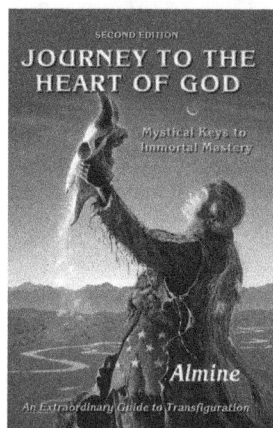

Journey to the Heart of God

Second Edition

Mystical Keys to Immortal Mastery

Ground-breaking cosmology revealed for the first time, sheds new light on previous bodies of information such as the Torah, the I Ching and the Mayan Zolkien. The explanation of man's relationship as the microcosm as set out in the previous book A Life of Miracles, is expanded in a way never before addressed by New Age authors, giving new meaning and purpose to human life. Endorsed by an Astro-physicist from Cambridge University and a former NASA scientist, this book is foundational for readers at all levels of spiritual growth.

Published: 2009, 276 pages, soft cover, 6 x 9, ISBN: 978-1-934070-26-0

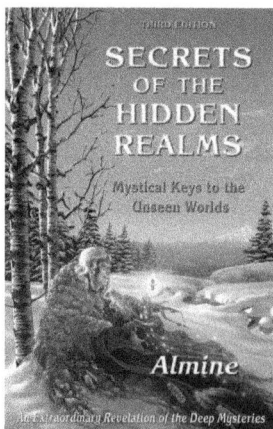

Secrets Of The Hidden Realms

Third Edition

Mystical Keys to the Unseen Worlds

This remarkable book delves into mysteries few mystics have ever revealed. It gives in detail:
- The practical application of the Goddess mysteries
- Secrets of the angelic realms
- The maps, alphabets, numerical systems of Lemuria, Atlantis, and the Inner Earth
- The Atlantean calender, accurate within 5 minutes
- The alphabet of the Akashic libraries.

Secrets of the Hidden Realms amazing bridge across the chasm that has separated humanity for eons from unseen realms.

Published: 2011, 412 pages, soft cover, 6 x 9, ISBN: 978-1-936926-38-1

Other Books by Almine

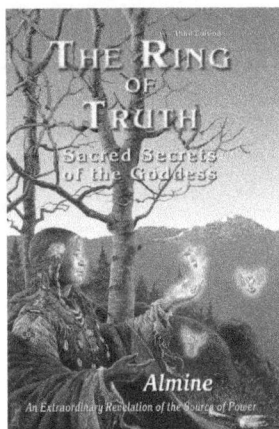

The Ring of Truth

Third Edition

Sacred Secrets of the Goddess

As man slumbers in awareness, the nature of his reality has altered forever. As one of the most profound mystics of all time, Almine explains this dramatic shift in cosmic laws that is changing life on earth irrevocably. A powerful healing modality is presented to compensate for the changes in the laws regarding energy that healers have traditionally relied upon. The new principles of beneficial white magic and the massive changes in spiritual warriorship are meticulously explained.

Published: 2009, 260 pages, soft cover, 6 x 9, ISBN: 978-1-934070-28-4

Music by Almine

Children of the Sun

Music from the Known Planets (Re-mastered and re-titled version of the Interstellar Sound Elixirs) The beautiful interstellar sound elixirs received and sung by Almine.

Price $9.95 MP3 Download
$14.95 CD

Labyrinth of the Moon

Music from the Hidden Planets (Re-titled version of the Sound Elixirs of the Hidden Planets) All the vocals in these elixirs are received and sung in the moment by Almine

Price $9.95 MP3 Download
$14.95 CD

Jubilation – Songs of Praise

Music from around the world to lift the heart and inspire the listener. The extraordinary mystical quality of the music, and the exquisite clarity of Almine's voice, creates the ambient impression of being in the presence of angels.

Price $9.95 MP3 Download
$14.95 CD

Visit Almine's website www.spiritualjourneys.com for worldwide retreat locations and dates, online courses, radio shows and more. Order one of Almine's many books, CDs or an instant download. US toll-free phone: 1-877-552-5646

Many of Almine's books and online courses are available in other languages such as German, Russian, Spanish, French and Danish

www.ingramcontent.com/pod-product-compliance
Lightning Source LLC
Chambersburg PA
CBHW030526100426
42813CB00001B/160